Opening the *Island*

Opening the Island

Anne Compton

Fitzhenry & Whiteside

Opening the Island
Copyright © 2002 Fitzhenry & Whiteside

All rights reserved. No part of this book may be reproduced in any manner without the express written consent from the publisher, except in the case of brief excerpts in critical reviews and articles. All inquiries should be addressed to:

Fitzhenry and Whiteside Limited
195 Allstate Parkway
Markham, Ontario L3R 4T8

In the United States:
121 Harvard Avenue, Suite 2
Allston, Massachusetts 02134

www.fitzhenry.ca   godwit@fitzhenry.ca

Fitzhenry & Whiteside acknowledges with thanks the Canada Council for the Arts, the Government of Canada through its Book Publishing Industry Development Program, and the Ontario Arts Council for their support of our publishing program.

National Library of Canada Cataloguing in Publication Data

Compton, Anne
    Opening the island

Poems.
ISBN 1-55041-638-3

    I. Title.

PS8555.O5185O64   2002   C811'.6   C2002-901048-9
PR9199.4.C65O64   2002

U.S. Cataloguing-in-Publication Data

Compton, Anne.
    Opening the island / Anne Compton. — 1st ed.
[104] p. : cm.

ISBN 1-55041-638-3 (pbk.)

1. Canadian poetry — 20th century. I. Title.
811.5/ 408   21   CIP PR9199.3.C66   2002

Cover design and text typesetting: Kinetics Design & Illustration

Cover art: Details from *Twilight Cousin's Shore PEI*, 1999, Oil glaze, 30 x 40, by Tony Diodati (website: www.tonydiodati.com)

Printed and bound in Canada

For
Lydia Jardine Compton
In Memory

And for Aaron and Quentin, my sons

Contents

	Acknowledgements	ix
1	At the Bridge the Body Rises	1
2	Women Writing Men	19
3	Inherit the Light	39
4	Body my house / my horse my hound ...	59
5	Closing the Island	77
	Index of titles	87
	Notes	91

Acknowledgements

Editors of the following journals kindly provided space for first publication of some of my poems, sometimes in earlier versions.
Canadian Literature: "Tidying the Tower: The Lady of Shalott Without Tennyson"
Dalhousie Review: "Men and Women, Remembered"
Descant: "Unreadable Flowers," "Amanuensis: John Milton's Daughter," "rooms," and "Waking"
Fiddlehead: "Island Graveyard," "Inherit the Light," "Convolvulus," "Heat, August," "Sons and Lovers," "House on a Hill," "The Womb Lies Beneath the Heart," and "Tower: Poem for the Spoken Voice"
Malahat Review: "Letter to France," "Hester Pyrnne's Letter to Surveyor Pue," "She Talks to Pictures at an Exhibition Because the Curator Won't Allow Notes," "'The Mermaids Singing,'" "Guenevere Writes to Them Who Wrote of Her," "Lightwork in Vermeer," "Your House Should Be a Second Skin — Real Estate Ad," and "She Declines His Proposition"
The New Brunswick Reader: "plotted," "North Shore: PEI," "Cézanne: Still Life," "Claude Monet: *Rouen Cathedral, 1894*," "The Falling Asleep of the Virgin Mary," "This and That Room: June," "What Land Means, Autumn 1998," and "Done with the Compass / Done with the Chart"
Pottersfield Portfolio: "Ripening Grain"
Queen's Quarterly: "In the fall I remember"
Women's Review of Books (Wellesley College): "Nine Women Come for Dinner"

Island Magazine (Australia) and *The New Brunswick Reader* re-printed some of the above poems. A number of these poems were broadcast on "Live Poets," CBC Radio; others appear in the CBC documentary *The Islanders*. Eight of these poems appeared in the mixed media exhibition *You Think of Houses*. 9 April — 28 May, 2000. The Space Gallery. Saint John, NB.

Editors of three anthologies generously included my work:
Following the Plow: Recovering the Rural — "In the fall I remember" and "What Land Means, Autumn 1998"
Landmarks: An Anthology of New Atlantic Poetry of the Land — "Ripening Grain" and "plotted"
New Canadian Poetry — "Lightwork in Vermeer," "Unreadable Flowers," and "'The Mermaids Singing'"
The New Brunswick Arts Board, through a Creation Grant, enabled me to work on this book. George Elliott Clarke, Maria Kubacki, and Ross Leckie supported me in my grant application, and in other important ways.
To Pat Joas, Bob Moore, and my son Aaron, who have read these poems many times, I am particularly indebted. To my brothers and sisters, whose familial love is gratefully acknowledged in some of these poems, thank-you.

It was a great pleasure to work with Evan Jones, editor of the manuscript, whose guidance was offered with such tact and grace.

1

At the Bridge the Body Rises

And we start, with a new and terrible energy,
to write the poems of the imagined real place.

Robert Kroetsch

North Shore, PEI

Who knows? Perhaps they walk the beaches in their
    long-belted dresses,
the Island women of long ago.
Possibly, we will see them, in a lucent spell of light,
    tidal pacing leisurely,
an assemblage through the surf.
Their hair come loose from its combs — though it's whipped
    by the wind — is left unattended
as they perambulate the coast.
They're absorbed in telling over lives lived inland past the dunes.
Doubtless, it's of the fields that they're speaking
or a cairn that stood there once.
And the men whose fieldwork's finished
sleep on: solaced by the sea-sounding speech of women naming men.
It's not for the living
they slow-step through the swell with their heads bent together
and their skirts stiff with salt.
Every birth begins a story and the story as they tell it defies
the tumbled silence of stone.

If we saw, could we hear, in the interval of the wave, what ghost
tells to ghost
so coolly now passion's past.

What they know must be as limitless as the sea (vocal)
that rolls to Europe
off the Island's North Shore.

Men and Women, Remembered

The cool rooms of summer houses
fern plants casting shadows
down a long hallway
sideboards and banisters
    the women, the washing folded in their arms.

    And down in the dusty yard —
    shoploft, well-house,
    pumproom. Words
    unused, unsung, in me
    and the singing of the men.

plotted

Here is a place you live on
[everywhere else you live in]   *in* Ontario they say,
she lives *on* the island.
Alighted, they mean, but the locution is unfamiliar.

Here, where spire and silo define a hypotenuse with
the sea, and so it is with hills,
every sea-surrounded hour   reminder enough
of how temporary
habitation here.

[someone is walking the long rows of a field inspecting a crop
his arms clasped behind his back: wind-braced
an acquired habit
his garment resembles clothes]

Should illusions of permanence beset you some late spring day
while they're setting out the bedding plants, looking forward,
a few steps to the shore will remind you
how brief, fugitive, the spell of weather here.

[also, the opposite is true
here they live on — into a future unguessed]

Inland, quiltwork hills, chesspiece houses and barns
tucked into a corner of yard
clumps of birch and softwood contoured to a hill
every field bordered at roadside by lupine and queen anne's lace

its symmetry, the craft of a quick-speaking story-teller
who'd have you know such places are prologue to a tale

fences, whether wire or wood or stone, slope down to vastness
shoreline of the possible: a double rhythm of the mind.

On the return ferry, the visitors say, it reminded me
so much of Ireland, the lowlands, Camelot, some place
I've been or dream I've been
[silted in memory, insinuated in books, ancestral]
lending library to the restive, hospitable to loss
open, an opening

This and That Room, June

The candles are falling from
the Horse Chestnut tree. Soon it will be the longest day.
You want to be in all the rooms at once —
in the wainscotted dining room,
on the verandah with its curtain of convolvulus vine,
in the white room upstairs where blinds
filter brightness
but you are here in the cool enclosure of the Chestnut's limbs
so low-growing they trail leaves on the ground. *The good room,*
we called it back home. Cool on the hottest days,
distant from
kitchen and pantry (where imperceptibly flour
from the morning's baking floated on the air).
Its porcelain door knob, stonecold to the hand, knocks
on your spine. Something turns over in the body as you enter.
Even the colour of its words — maroon, organ, ottoman —
are of lower temperature. Must and drowsiness in them.
Dimmer the light here. Flickering leaf shadows
and the trellised vines on the carpet indistinguishable.
In glass-doored cupboards, in photo-albums,
sepia ancestors on thick black paper.
Thick-bearded men upright in armchairs, women to the rear. Children
dead soon after the poised moment,
before the rectangular black box, gazing placidly
at someone, something, beyond the perimeter.
Who braided, plaited, her hair for the last time,
this girl forever equanimous in the good room
where time and the intemperate do not intrude
and where it is always the solstitial day.

4 April, 1991

Snow in April should not surprise us
nor should the death of an old man past eighty

whose patrimony is the air of his absence.

April days succeed to sunshine
my father will return no more.

A patriarch they called him
the last of the line of wisehearted men.
We who survive him are not his successors:
the river and woods, the fields and the hills —
these were his.

He will walk no more in his garden by the birch wood
nor gather the bruised and beautiful apples from dewy grass.
His sons will not seek him, nor
his daughters, returning, settle by his side.

Every season will be telling his absence —
the earth will extol him in fruitfulness,
in gold and green, the crops will salute him.

Earth and grove, where he was magnificent, will remember him.

ploughshares into words

Last of eleven; born into loss
late to the childhoods of brothers and sisters
always ahead. Knowing stuff. "Sophie, what does *perpetual* mean?"

From the steps, our mam calling *John 'n Anne, supper.*
Calling us in from the fields or the shop. The orchard, where
we roll Red Astrakans, Russets, Courtlands into a barrel.

Tipping the turnips down a cellar hatch
into winter. The cellar where weather
doesn't reach. What can't be preserved there?

Look-alikes in plaid and durable cloth. Handed down.
Me in his clothes. His skin. Almost the same size. Could be
twins. What we all are, I'm hoping, so I'll know what they know.

Winter's for words when
the real work's been done. House-banked books.
Someone is talking about the Battle of Inkerman

like it was yesterday. I might catch up. Make it to
Libbie, eldest of eleven, if I listen.

2

The horse canters, the light sleigh behind. John 'n me wrapped
in the buffalo robe. Only his breathing. Memorize that.

In the barn, my father singing the psalms under his breath.
Hay bales opening like books while he hums. Music and song
not allowed at church. A schism has set us apart, a family

speaking in tongues out of turn. The precentor
gives out the line, the rest follow. The drone of it.
Not like the words that get things done. *Insurrection*
is a word I heard on the radio.

My father says the word *poetry* the way he says *fadder*.
His own, long dead before I was born. A tone of reserve
for the dead and the holy. Every forkful of hay lifted up.

I follow him in from the night.
The warming oven where we dry our gear, what the world was.

Amanuensis: John Milton's Daughter

When my father died I was born
into my own language.
Short phrases, throbbing like blood
beat, like shoe sound on parquetry —
hurrying away. Long phrases
lying lazily in odoriferous sunshine, away from
the damp room of his weepy blank eye
the blank verse narrative I walked to
up and down, it seemed, a hundred halls,
so he could hear back the rhythm of his line.
Wrote, read, walked to his measure.
Woman's body in male syntax
under order
odour of
clipped hedges and disciplined vines: his text.
We can, Deborah, shed the snakeskin
go upright again
oxygenate the verb.

The Dinner Party

I want to get back to —
        a tree-lined lane
        tall poplars obscuring a housefront
        the stone steps
        the inside / outside porches
        — where I came from

the kitchen, its familiar furnishings, patterned
linoleum, the long table, my father at its head,
brothers and sisters, the bustle
of mealtime, my mother mid-way between pantry and
table, the youngest, her place nearest my mother.

It can't not be. All of that.
Somewhere there are single days I could visit.
Almost, I know how to get there:

a road lying parallel to the one I am on if I could see.

So that suddenly among low-growing brush and thin-stemmed trees
an opening, a lane,
ah, so there it is
as if it had always been there: that feeling
upon arrival of its having been so simple really.
Like the friend's directions to a dinner party
which seemed so complicated but when followed
so elementary, so perfectly clear.

In relief — home at last — I hurry forward
the long lane, the familiar trees, the stone steps.

They are pulling back their chairs
settling in.
So many. I had forgotten we were so many —
the family likeness from face to face
and among them, the unexpected guest.
Who is this stranger who sits nearest my mother, privileged
place of the youngest, the stranger whose face, not unlike the others,
bears no welcome.
Who sits where I should sit?

She will not have me here. I have come, she says,
the wrong day. I say the way though was long and hard
and I belong. "Did," she says, "Begone."

October Morning

Down in the garden   hoar frost has fallen;
my children play on trails they have made.
The youngest   my daughter
holds in her hand what cannot be held.

I should tell her—
It's not real. It's not even snow.
I should warn my foolish, excitable daughter.

I had no daughter.
The memory is old grey and wrong.
I was the daughter and
she never warned me.

Hoar frost is such a lie.

Island House, November

I am on this road   out of season
brought back
by a summer neighbour's death.

It is a foolish dare, some poet said,
to look upon one's own house
closed up for winter:
iron lock upon the door
invites a nightmare
rebukes
careless unnoticing summer days.

The teacup I carried into the garden
that summer day I walked with you
will fill with snow. You were so sure

birds fledged in the leafiest trees.

Now in the bare tree
the abandoned nest: darkness at the curve of a branch.

Such a stupid confidence
in birds and trees
and family.

Going Over the Sand Dunes

Shame said the sand whirling like a dervish in the wind
Hurt, as you have hurt, said the marram grass, spiky

and deep-rooted on the dune. A pity
about your bleeding feet, but you knew the path.

Away hissed the waves sliding round the pebbles,
and under roared the breakers crashing on the sand bar
a distance from the shore.

All will be well, well, intoned the ocean
carrying its cargo to the deep.

>Sun was wan, wind skittish,
>not a soul on the shore.

That wind sall blaw for evermair.

Night Drive, November, for her ninetieth birthday

In the pitch
of a narrow Island road, return trip,

I know now I've led the wrong life.

Somewhere in the darkness there's a house I didn't live
sons and daughters lost in the hallways
a man with a lantern crossing the space between my voice and his,
shielding the glass with a free hand.

A poplar tree, bent by a north shore gale, tipped
forever toward a second storey window where maybe a bed waits.
Its branches scrape on the pane, like a bird wantin' in
you could hear him say.

"Two, two-fifty, to the acre": the crops he offered
same day he asked, "Is it twelve on Sunday? Can we count on noon?"

That was after his father gave us the house, land and all.

There used to be a ferry that *sailed on the hour* as if time
not the sea floated you away. I took the eleventh
savvy gulls circling the deck, deft thieves of the bread trail.

A gifted woman, she's lived in the one house
a whole life.

2

Women Writing Men

There are no categories for what I know....

Elizabeth Jennings

We are not really at home in our interpreted world.

Rainer Maria Rilke

Letter to France

> *This day is call'd the feast of Crispian....*
> Henry V

She wrote him on St. Crispin's Day. Come
safe home (your grace) dear cousin. The child
stirs in his sleep, safe within the walls
of my womb. The castle is chill
for the festival while you are away.
And I must be up and going when the New Year shows.
We who belong to you will be as the mist and the rain
everywhere, unsettled, subtle, until
the Sun returning dispel disgrace and
dower the double blood made one.

And we will call him Dudley
for the fair field where we lay on Lammas Day.
Or, if my King does not come home, I'll call him Abelard
for lost.

Hester Pyrnne's Letter to Surveyor Pue

        I send you this epistle by courier Time,
addressed fourscore years in the future, land not so
remote that words can't reach you. What I couldn't say here,
and fear will be intercepted, I beg you pass along.
Included, please find, the mouldered object, whose golden filaments,
hardly gold even now, sprang like syllables on
the gate-legged letter they made me wear. Gate to a garden
proscribed, where roses irrepressible (one time, I plucked)
flourish. No matter the gate, the rose once ripe cannot revert,
experienced must be expressed: vermilion ecstasy
wrought by the fingertips.

        Permit, dear Pue, this gold thread
— attar of rose, converted to chapel alphabet, and worn —
to pass your custom. Publish. Burnish the gold,
lest (haw, haw) some spiny shrub spreading
o'erwhelm the garden known in the fingertips.

She Talks to Pictures at an Exhibition Because the Curator Won't Allow Notes

They knew light, those French painters, rendered ruthlessly
the unloved face of the absinthe drinker:
Illumination laid on like this sobers sentiment. Have another drink,
dear lady. There is a loveliness in cloudy liquid,
as in the biased light of memory.
A quick draught, and then another, will restore
— turn to your companion, insist he see —
the firmer outline, the warm flesh tones, you're certain of.

No more charming than this November day,
the sails at Argenteuil, but memory, that artful auditor,
wears chromatic glasses in the unforgiving light.

"The Mermaids Singing"

Dear Mr. Prufrock, could you manage tea Wednesday week.
It's the shuttered house on the hill where the road curves.
I believe you've been (nearby) before.
Cousin Frances, the lepidopterist, is with us for the month.
Of course, she hasn't brought the collection
but she loves to talk. Some says she's sibyllic.
The usual, including Bixie and Freddie, will be here.
Mind the dogs on the stair as you approach. (Daddy is so silly
about the dogs since he bought that disagreeable little
    drawing *Salome*.)
They'll drag the least thing down: *ungart'red,*
and down-gyved to his ankle — all's bare.
I hope you'll be firm. Yours, Cordelia Merman.

Guenevere Writes to Them Who Wrote of Her

I have been before, you know, spoken of, remarked.
Chosen subject of many men it seems.
Good Queen, bad Queen, as fit their fancy.

In Malory and Morris brocade-bound (voluptuous folds of fabric)
so high-dressed to be *despoiled into her smock*. Shriven and burned.
Majesty set to shame and stake: unwholesome womanhood in
    the muggy air.
Feet feeling for the first time, the muddy earth
and in my mouth, the taste of ash. Acrid as printer's ink.

And that other, the heavy-lidded laureate, who had me grovelling
at my lord's feet, sheltering sin within white arms and loosened hair.
I never thought to. The court was never in my keeping.
These hands are flesh, my lords, not cups for a court's roundness.
Not within my handspan, the making and unmaking of his knights.
Blame me not for that. No more did I betray
the goodly King: his heart was not given.

Heart and court he kept far from me, except I ornamented both.
Sorry I am that both were broken, but by Christ's law,
he set me on to my soul's damnation: Or else,
I found that path myself though still he loved me not.

                Bestowed on one so high, so good
(such a woman for such a man, they said), complement to a king.
Those thick dark brows so sternly met, how could I jest?
His chaste kiss rebuked my warmth, my wit,

my memory of red-roofed pavilions, green-roofed avenues,
and at my side the King's ambassador
caparisoned in his golden-shafted courtesy.

And after that, how fit the ceremony — holy words —
    to heart's desire?
I bent the words. This, not the other — love's revelry — was my sin.
And so it was I reasoned:
as Maundy's bread and wine are blessed to serve for Easter morn,
so by the marriage sacrament (was I) pre-sanctified for Lancelot.
I compromised Christ to my longing: bought terms
of pleasure with holy writ.
Bethought me the very Mass prepared. Analogy most pernicious.
It served. Arthur was my King, Lancelot my gracious Knight,
allegiance easy.

This black-spotted blasphemy no one
not even Agravain, and his successor spies, espied.
They looked into my heart (they thought) and called it
lust, this goodly love.
What God bestows, He intends; it needed not
the sacramental dress I artfully connived:
Iniquity imperishable in a courtyard fire.

What no man wrote being with courts and kings concerned.

*Done with the compass, /
Done with the chart.*

> *Emily Dickinson*

Whether at Haworth or Amherst
they were all islanders — those writing women —
living far off the mainland, they
knew dangerous seas by swimming

        no vessel rigged and fitted
        no mother map for them
        for compass, eyes and ears and flesh

breathed an element others navigated,
struck syllables off submerged continents.

Tidying the Tower:
The Lady of Shalott without Tennyson

I did not want to be awakened
called from cloth to casement

when he stepped into my mirror, a fire
plumed in my body

from frame to frame he filled its space
till space existed for his resplendent bearing

his unbearable light put out the world
emptied me of the pictured landscape

>   back then, I never could tell
>   what in the mirror was me, the room, or the world

>   two small boys, their red bonnets bobbing
>   among yellow leaves: saw all from above, my perspective

>   around a topography of hills and distance
>   my hair grew briary, seasons unfolded over my face

>   one winter a herd of deer stepped
>   delicately over the frozen river

>   their soft nubile horns nudged
>   velvety through my threads

the sight of him cracked my gaze:
sickened of sight, I wanted touch

stones crumbled under the weight
of my longing, the pattern unravelled

small boys bled on the flagstone floor
deer crashed through ice

tidied the tower, twigs from my hair, swept up
bits of mirror, spread

tapestries on the floor to lie on
a glittering professional, he did not turn back

up there, I'd said, *this blue for the water*:
it must have been a trick of the light, effect of distance
in here it's more like grey and ever so swift

Rheumatic Fever:
any nineteenth-century poet to her mentor

And, looking on myself, I seemed not one / For such man's love!
Elizabeth Barrett Browning

I would have exchanged Eden's air
for your exhaled breath.
A desperate respirator, I yearned toward
the oxygen intoxication of your mouth, inhalation
of elysium weather: ether sucked to the lung.

                A physician of sorts, you
prescribed a course of reading   recommended
the second-hand breath of your books
— even autographed your most recent volume —
a remote respiration
to be carried to a sick bed
while heart valves heal.

Tower: Poem for the Spoken Voice

Because women in the upper storeys demand a face at the pane....
                                             W.B.Yeats

The odd time, voices float up from the river
voices I shouldn't be able to hear since sailboats,
at this distance, look like so many lazy summer swans.
Still, all the serious things happen on the water, or so I'm told.
Not much truck on the river road, a quagmire in spring,
hot stones under foot in summer, the grocery boy says.
Farriers with their gear. Pedlars.
I wouldn't crack a window for that traffic.
When I was little, I was allowed to go down to the milkroom.
In England, where I've never been, they call it a dairy.
I know that, and other things, from books.
In the separator bowl, the cream rose to the top.
And the milk ran blue and thin from the spout below.
I guess Daddy's tower is a kind of cream separator.
We're on top: three auburn daughters — roses and cream.
I'm the eldest. "Quick as a fox," Daddy likes to brag.
"Fox in a cage," I say, but Daddy doesn't know about books.
Doesn't know that after a real hot day, there are layers of air
at different temperatures. Sound gets bent and you hear
what you shouldn't be able to hear — the voices of men on boats.
Air freight. Saying bales and wharves and friggin' custom.
Shoutin' a blue fury like Zeus. Not what you'd expect from a swan.
One time a swan — Do you know this story? — freighted a
    woman away.
Her thighs caressed by the dark webs: That'd be one way of leaving.
Someone would be sure to get wind of it, what with the way
certain currents of air affect the transmission of sound.

Can you imagine the uproar in the tower? Daddy listening in. Serve him right. Though a fox, I'd say, is liable to eat a swan. Suits me. I'm thin as air.

Sound and light, that's what I think of most days. Wave vibration. And I'm not talking about seaman. Though Clara does. "Men go down to the sea in ships / Wives lean out the window in slips," she's always saying. Freak occurrences of wind or heat, I tell her, give preferential treatment to sound and light — to their conveyance. Clara doesn't care. She doesn't know what I'm planning.

Nine Women Come For Dinner

The women I know have sons.

Prandial and festive we gather
a carnival crowd of happy hags
free of husbands and lovers
— and talk about our sons —
even their failures charm us.
Oh the stories we tell — competing maternal narratives.

When my own sons come home, at some late hour,
we show — do not have to say —
the men have come in.

Pairs

> Shortage of organs forces medical transplant team to resort to pigs.
> Newscast Item

If in a family of eleven, there were ten prodigals
how many fatted calves would the parents need
and how long would the party last?

But wait, would a daughter returning
merit anything more than a scrawny hen, a cast-off
cloak, a minor trinket?
Say she'd gone amuck, like the prodigal,
would there be any welcome at all?

After running
through the money
would she find field-work the way the second-best brother did?

For her, as for him, would forking the swine pods
inspire thoughts of home: better a servant in my father's house etc. etc.

Not likely.
She'd have eaten the swine pods, enlarged the piggery.

(Who's telling this story, anyway?)

A frequent feeder, she'd grow plump and rosy, her little feet
barely visible beneath the smock. Prodigious size, her sin

alas, alack, how spoiled she is

(It's not funny to pick on a pig in a parable, and probably profane,
but so it is for the haggard sister who stayed at home. Is *she*
  the narrator?)

which sets me to thinking about Mary and Martha, spendthrift and
dutiful daughter. How pairs permeate. Like Enkidu and Gilgamesh
wild and civil, a pair made whole. The stray always comes in.

Now there's a man, who without pause, would've eaten
the swine pods. Enkidu in his younger years
before his better-half
dreamed another self and summoned him from the field.
St. Augustine, it is said parenthetically, stole some pears
he didn't want and fed them to the pigs. Would Eve, you have to
wonder, have pitched the apple had pigs been standing by? Bent

the story out of shape.

How they figure our gluttony.
I mean *if pigs had wings*, they wouldn't serve.

Closest to us, it turns out. Our new pairing.
Taking them to heart after all.

The shape of things to come: the old goes

if in a family of eleven, everyone has his opposite, her
completion, who was hers being last, leftover, eleventh?
Without a better brother, a steadfast sister, what chance
regaining the garden?

The Poet in His Cell

He inflects   the word *blouse* just so
a slow un-doing   of small buttons

vatic utterance
a voltaic cell that shifts the charge to me.

I'll believe anything for a spell.

Your kindness, he says, with episcopal courtesy,
*is a Saint Martin's summer, unexpected weather
to one mewed up.* So mild in his way. Convincing too.

After an unseasonable six-day's clemency
the sun is a hard cold light
emptying the word *woman* of illusion.

Do Not Write Any More

love foregone lives on

a lit lamp in a cupboard, bolted
dangerous

yet in that room where the cupboard is
light leaks out
                      though no one says
                      they see

over there years away by water or whatever
the everyday things you're doing
have my notice, my part
passed into flame

3

Inherit the Light

> Perhaps we are *here* in order to say: house,
> bridge, fountain, gate, pitcher, fruit-tree, window....
>
> *Rainer Maria Rilke*

Lightwork in Vermeer

No one knows why the light in Delft is different from everywhere
nor why the women in Vermeer stitch and pour, make lace and music,
write and receive letters   weigh air
in concentrated stillness.

And though the critic remarks "the restrictive ordinariness
of his subject matter," meaning the women's work, where but here,
"in two smallish rooms," might miracle occur?

The windows of Vermeer open inward
letting eternity flow over a sill
in parody of earthlight.

Not earthly, at all, the dispersal of light
that through a north-facing window retrieves
The Milkmaid from time, ennobles
the bread, the jug, and the wicker. Converts
the fluid to forever.

In almost every painting (in all, fewer than forty)
the women, gentle and disbelieving, turn to us,
"You did not know," they say or will say:
the spoken and the unspoken being the same in this light.

They wear their vestments — lemony yellow, ultramarine blue —
like stonework. These women who cannot age.
The merit of pearls is theirs also: touches of opalescent white
without outline.

The Woman with the Scales ignores the pearls scattered before her
— a lapidary lapse brought on by light
her uplifted arm welcomes
the heft of light on her limbs
weighable radiance
the illuminated white of the hood and the smock enfold her
away

In the viscid air, the gestures of the women slow and halt,
become masonry.

By the windows of Vermeer, light is suspensive.

Ripening Grain

(*Crows over the Cornfields*, Van Gogh, 1890)

Remember how we caught hell for running
through the grainfield.
Three, four, of us burst upon that golden grove,
fanning out in a forest of grain.

The game was to slide silently through the pliable stalks
      surprise the enemy and pounce.
Pack of hooligans my father said and threshed us out.

By then, we'd initialled the hundred-acre field
in loopy letters of flattened grain that spelled
our giddy guilt: birds thriving on the damage.

When the combine came, we hid in the culvert
      cursed the end-of-the-world rumble
that converted our silk-sounding paradise to stubble field.

Nothing emptier than a stubble field in fall,
the Van Gogh crows circling. Unless it's this:
the ripening world you abruptly left, spelling
in stone your traitorous names.

The Falling Asleep of the Virgin Mary: August 15

We rode, that summer, through anhydrous nights
like shipboard travellers. Dreams
were deep and of the dead. The still
of day, the stir of night, afflicted us.
August began in June and steadily climbed red skies:
calendars bleached, barometry declined. We forgot
the meaning of *before* and *after*.

We are the cargo of the dead's dreaming.

In gusty darkness, houses shuddered from foundations,
miraged in morning mist, or facsimiles did,
nailed, once more, by heat to habit. We led our lives inside,
inside draped light. Reality leaked away like well water
receding underground. Pitchers stood empty.

Someone will do with us indescribable things.

Cézanne: Still Life

Allowance must be made for the hat-maker's son
(allowance grudgingly given, by lies received — a father's stipend).
A shaggy man, he shook off affection, escaped
their clutch on the sleeve of his soul, yet dreamed
the curves of women meeting the curves of hills
the elegant alphabet of God spelling in light and colour.

Able to see shifting shapes
forever creating one another, stumbled alone.
In others' work the autopsy of a dead world, in Cézanne's the living.

For such eyes, he traded a little life. God's cruel joke —
impair the sighted; hearts to the blind.

Blinded by the Word

Why is *next year* a foreign country whose language and habits
we do not know?
Won't the cats be yawning in the green chair, same as now,
the kids the same but bigger?
We carry the language kit to the past, exchange maudlin words
about old ruins,
but for the city on the plain, whose citizens bustle about
(ourselves among them), we haven't a word.

Why is it there are words a-plenty to tell the past, but no words
for next year?
Sure there are calendars, train tickets, architect's plans
from three angles,
but we don't even try to greet the descendant-
strangers. Can't get a word past midnight.
Waiting for the future to come, is it shyness or fear
keeps us back?

2

When Babel fell, the plain went blank.
Bricks clattered to the ground, a chaotic disorder. This,
they said, is the past and refused to look over the wreck.
Neighbouring days — out there on the plain — shimmered and sank,
or so they thought, mistaking speech for sight, blinded by the word.

As if it was a word in a foreign language, they whispered *tomorrow*
around fires behind rubble.
Their cousin's speech was a confusion to them, and she went out
on the plain. Her name was Eve. In a city, in a far country,
she minds a fruit stand. The apples
are brick red and delicious.

A Thin Woman Looks at Renoir's The Bathers 1918–19

Those glittering fat girls, your *Bathers*, indolently
staring me down: last painting of an arthritic old man.

Culmination of a life time, you quietly concluded, and died,
joining those others — men, I mean — for whom the ample
Venus beckoned frame by frame: classic pose of erotic desire.

Dearest empiricist, how shall I understand your desertion?
Comprehend the fantastical amplitude, alien to my angular life?

A boy from Limoges, you ornamented vases at the porcelain works
pellucid round shapes reclining in the palm of one hand:
enough money and evenings at the Louvre with the old masters.

Summers later, colours scumbling over one another in the
    Seine sunshine
of your landscapes — and you were not satisfied. Shape you missed.

Tore up the transcriptions of the moment, began your bathers.
From the mind, through the hand: beyond tyranny of eye.

"Flowers," you said, with your final breath. Not of this world.

Shall I vilify your crippled longing? Or, close my eyes also?

Unreadable Flowers

When Catharine Parr Traill met Ophelia at the brookside
she gave the brooding naturalist a talking-to.
Your alphabet of flowers, my good girl,
will not spell here. It's a cold climate.
Serviceable shoes and notions, that's what's wanted.
Sensibility tends to derangement and aimless
wandering. Not so long ago, Fancy starved here
for just that reason
though flowers — edible in all shades but yellow — make
"marvellous food" and serve sundry uses, as for instance:
the stamen of the *Ranunculaceae* is long and hooded
[very forward, you can't miss it]
its pollen, if carefully collected, yields a prophylactic.
In spring, the root — of Monkshood or nun's habit — prevents
    conception.
Although for this, proper footwear will serve.
Also good for wading.

Heat, August

The day lilies refused to have their day
folded their trumpets, furled their orange peal.
No wind stirred the basil air: Odour and colour drew in,
drew down, to white roots fingering earthdamp rocks.

In shuttered houses
siesta sleepers, lightly sheeted,
sought the lowest rooms. Dreamed flight from.
The red giant sulked in the sky above, expanded and contracted
in a white rage, vowed a dwarfish revenge.
Calla lilies for cinder earth.

2

Wind moving at the speed of light: the crab pulsar,
spinning still, has shock in it.
Light years have not restored *strong, level flight*,
nor recovered the derelict dust that exploding
fell into time and language
detritus of fallen far-distant motion.

Claude Monet: Rouen Cathedral, Early Morning, 1894

The dissolution of form in colour, you saw, in the everyday air
and motion everywhere.
Taught us to see tender blue in the darkest shadow. Told us more.

Painter of light, you put out certitude. Awakening
us to light-borne vanishings,
your impression
emptied the cathedral of custom.

Though at Giverny, you sat down to lunch at eleven everyday
— a clockwork household.

Host

Are you sometimes wildly disturbed at night? Darkness
not coming down fast enough.

                Wind whining
round a window: all your memories
met together and beating at the pane.
It's you they want, those glossy black creatures
                          winged symbionts
of a light you cannot extinguish.

And this is the meaning of *Let your light so shine*:
a host's phosphorescence. Past things
swarm in the night. Making a shambles.

        2

Out there in the garden witch weather
ratting up
the arrangement of flowerbeds: pyrethrum
and phlox going down in flames.
Combustible herbary.

Nothing you can name lasts:
everywhere larvae beneath the leaf.

Crow Song, November

All-over grey sky, heavy on the tallest trees.
Dirt-sifting crows wrench their heads around

give me a swift sideways glance.

I'm so low-down
gravity's got its arms open to me.

There are better beds. I've been through them all.
Danced the dance. They're through with me.

So, what else from down here?

Leafless poplar scrub
looks a purple congregation   hazy, hymnless
though farmers, withdrawn from the fields, nurse a snug hope.
Fall plowing supposes spring. Just imagine.

Their fresh-turned furrows are frosted at the crest,
a chirpy look if you care for that sort of thing.

A certain notion of roof's come unhinged.

Crows know all the words from caul to crypt.

I look up   the most difficult ones
the most difficult like *murk* have the least definition.

Whiskey Jack fix me
with your beady eye.

Overall words don't matter   even the last one

it's the kiss of
                 the grounds keeper.

Mind Winter

Before bed a woman lifts an arm, unloosens a curtain
against the too bright snowfields.

All January is in her reach.

A few steps from her flannel asylum
scalded milk cools in a chipped cup.

Daylight hours gust from the roof trough.

Rage, a small dog she unleashes
afternoons. Puts down at nightfall.

Winter is a near-sleep, a shuffle
through landscapes so foreign
we close eyes, doors, the future against them.
Further cannot be seen.

On the broad river, hardened between hills,
figures no more real than Hansel and Gretel
pretend familiarity with strangeness.
The sugar-house, they hope, a small rising away.

Swirling snow / a broth flecked with red.

On Epiphany, the woman stopped reading. Nothing showed.
The mind in winter, she'd say, is on its own. On retreat.
Sensation cannot be validated.

Just as well. All of them are muffled.
Dormant as fish floored
beneath an overhead of ice.

rooms

the bed invites you, invites,   you
want to enter its invisible dark pooling   going on
between white covers, it smuggles seductions to you
down hallways, its whispers are heard in kitchens
  only in me in me can you give over, give up, go under
it is what you never want to leave river away from everyday
you think, this night will carry me far enough from cavemouth
light   once seen   hauls you again   out into living-
rooms furnished with time
pieces, mantle pieces, fire
floors where light is erected
and the word worshipped

templum
call that living if you like
come, put out the porchlight

4

Body my house
my horse my hound
what will I do
when you are fallen....

May Swenson

Your House Should Be a Second Skin

Real Estate Ad

Let me tell you what it's like. It's
like this. I'm running up the stairs
on some chore or other. And your mouth, your hands.

Night and its colossal desires enter the house
through windows and doors propped wide.

When the heart keeps open house, everything's
on the outside. As if love ever stayed. Or stilled.

A real state, it is, when a house resists
the drag of foundation and shingles sholom
the heart-felt house with clapping.

              In the inside out

Jane Austen novels

              spill from the shelves.

Serviceable shoes walk off.

Eros taking a second lease.

House on a Hill

The nails in the house have heaved. And what was
stable, shifts in the wind. Like those strike-anywhere
match-stick houses I built with my brother long ago.
Every breath liable to excite collapse. The loser
the one who brought the house down. *Don't exhale*,
I'd whisper, *or you'll be the worse for it*. These days
I expect to find the house on the hill in kindling.
Your love drains iron from bones. A deep frost,
it lifts nails from wood. You have housed me
in imminent breakdown, but I'll be the one
to walk away. Remember the story of the children.
One time, I struck the house into flame. I'm a sore loser.
Still, he didn't breathe a word. Not a sweet air.

Come now, my love. Think about the relative force
of frost and fire. Exhilarate me slowly.

Sons and Lovers

I have laid the cloth for you. Arranged
ripe pears in a blue bowl. Made a bed.
Love is three syllables before sleep.

You had to see your mother, miles away. Eager
to do that duty and return to your real family
you said. Her skin tearing like tissue paper
from the drug. Imperilled bones breaking
on bed linen. What is real for her?
Woman on the outskirts.

After the call, I saw how the pears leant on the rim
of the blue bowl. Women in yellow flared skirts seated
on a circular bench. Their necks inclined. Stems raised
in a final salute.

Where I touched them, tomorrow, there will be a bruise.
Perfection is an hour, a night at most. Or not.
A woman shakes out the sheets over a bed
takes what's left of her life
in her arms.

Landfall at High Tide Leads to Stormsurge

weather forecast, October 1998

Nightlong the wind bawls and abates. For all the world
like the sound of the sea though I'm far inland and
from home. Likely less than two
on the Beaufort Scale

And my hand on the swell of your belly
rises and falls with your sleep
though you are now
where no storm makes landfall
no surge sucks from shore

so Atlantic an absence nupitals me.

Drained to indifference by this minor interior river
what weather could matter to me?

Tomorrow, for sure, some small havoc at the doorway.
It'll need brine for this cuticule of pain.

The Womb Lies Beneath the Heart

There was a child   too beautiful to bear
I could not call her down   be her way into the world.

Dear friend, do you ever think of that child
and the tall likeness of your ways she'd be to-day?

Can we give names to the unconceived?

I do not ask now about you and me, and the way
it went. But with the lilacs blooming by the porch

a stone turned and I heard a heart beat.
I thought of us in her, and her in me.

Usually, I do not hear a sound.
Speech is slow and small after such silence.

She Declines His Proposition

> *Of men, the married are most conceited.*
> Latin Proverb

For you, furniture arranges itself like staging
   and walls frame. You command space as if
      space were an equilateral triangle
         and you its apex.

Six days of seven, you are in this building
   subordinating architecture to stardom.
Who would have thought structure so personal?

   Joists, carrying beams, studs
 regroup when you enter. A conqueror
to the tented field is Thursday's impression.

(I am on the edge of the field camouflaged
   by grass. The wind, caesar, brightens
      the pennant on the peaked roof
         of your pavilion.)

Some days, spiral staircases, curved balconies
   shuffle themselves to pyramid.
On those days, you are as remote as a pharaoh.

Unseen I know you are here by the room's shift,
the corridors unexhaled breath. Not that I mind
      the adjacent angle.

Manikin, you bring the house down and re-
    story it. I'd invite you to mine
        but its age couldn't take
           the fabrication.

Features

> *Senior Citizen widower requires woman to cook and*
> *clean house. Willing to dig worms and cut bait.*
> *Must own boat and motor. Please send photo of boat.*
> Kennebecasis Valley Viewer, August 1999

Please find enclosed photo of boat. Though there's no denying
its peeling paint, cracked rowlocks, and flaky caulking,
the motor's dandy. It's not in the picture.
You'd have to be in the boat to hear how good my motor is.

You can see its name painted in red
down near the waterline. Been launched a thousand times.

In my day, I've found lots of worms. They're in everything.
Most often though I've been the bait. The men cut up some
awful when I slipped away. Then followed after. Born fools.

House falling down around you, is it? You're lucky
you have a house. I knew men spent ten years
under sail (and other things) trying to get home.

Housework and boat. I'm surprised you didn't ask
for a truck or a horse. This face you're looking at
made a horse's ass out of an army of men
who thought themselves heroes, left others a house in ruins.

If you're interested, Widower, take a look out the window.
I'm the boat on the lake you're asking for.

The Insomniac's Lighthouse

"I'm tired from way back," she said, carrying it
like a bundle, a load of kindling, before her.
Arms wrapped around herself as if its weight chilled.

"Nights I've never slept," she said, "stay with me,
dragging at my coat: fretful children kept from home,
their own beds. As if I ever denied their company, their claim on me.

I remember when a name could light a fire in me
shelter them and me to sleep. We slept in the future tense.
The youngest in the curve of my arm, the limbs
of the others flung over us like a shaft of light.

Large as a lookout it was, the one bed we'd rise from.

When a name withdraws
something like a coastline is lost
the one you'd been approaching
where a house, shutters open, looked out to sea.
The light would have been extraordinary on that promontory.

The stickpeople children draw have no face.
I'm looking to
put this bundle down."

Winter Dusk

no one should be out in it

sky sinking
behind frozen river
the godawful acreage of it
rim of red before collapse
suctions the heart

what forsaken must look like in Russia

unhappy countries are all alike

the houses clustered up there on the hill, the lights
of some coming on like melancholy

the forecaster's *below normal*
divining our chances
for what? Something as ordinary as theirs

and you, foreclosing on that, fled to England where maybe
the forsythia's blooming.

I am west (or is it east) of you
the country's name doesn't matter
either way, they say, dusk fell and it's final

this is what hopelessness looks like
light leaving snow ice chill

They Hold My Coat

The dead in this house are hanging around
time on their hands. It's not that they raise
heating bills or dust. Or raid the refrigerator.
Still, I've grown thin from their favours.

Down corridors they press their stories upon me.
Indiscrete as coathooks, they put themselves forward.

Stay here, they chorus when I reach for my coat.
It could be yours we're making or making over.

In a corner at evening their eyes admire my bones.
I'm hungry for their praise. They know this.
It's what they know best. Starving.

Wrist

If I open this white sheath
criss-crossed by fine blue lines

that sometimes throb like marconi
will I see the signalman's face, relieve his despair?

This is the part of the body where bone thins out.
Barely enough to secure the extravagant spread of the hand

so articulate compared to the mute impassive wrist:
bearer of bracelets, bloodlines, arterial secrets,

more vulnerable than breasts and thighs
more patient than the unkissed mouth.

Odd that we carry time   where the caged heart
relays its trouble or joy, cuffed from view or not.

(I have fallen in love with the wrists of strangers
seen a beloved between the competent hand and the cuff)

Who conceived that irony: tick by pulse,
heartstroke by steady stroke?

Extending — how tentatively — a hand to the world

taking the weight in the lift of it all, bare
unsheltered: *carpus* it's called, heart-
bearing bone. Heart at sea.

shoulder blades

Named for the butcher or war: mis-named.
Most likely wings before we landed
on this grubby patch, and shed what?

Feathered flight: the archangel's hope for
some colloquy with the gods? Ell-maimed,
expelled, we clothed remembrance. Were told to.

A secret reserved, kept back, glimpsed by others
on a hot summer's day. We all face forward,
denied our former beauty. Sight

confined to the fleshy front. Take off
your shirt — what you call, *your scapular*.
Let me see the scars. Taste salt on my tongue.

The Room Before

In the Anteroom, men in their overcoats
shouldering them off. Awkward as boys. Lovable.
The brass plate over the door hopes for gentlemen.

Across the foyer, in seraphic script, Ladies' Cloak-
room although they no longer wear them. A place to decide
how you'll be off. Like wings, before an entrance. Quickening.

In the room before, the men are dear, so dear.
The women, what tenderness in their bare arms.

(Are there, you have to wonder, after-rooms? Wards, perhaps.)

I am, you will have noticed, a theorist of rooms.
Or dreamer.

In the one about the house, I make a return visit
not to the family home, a sprawl of rooms and levels,
but to the long low retirement of parents,
white, in a grove of birches. The house inset
as if in a picture book or stage set. The forethought
of ancestors: apple trees and lilacs drawing the grove near.

I travel west in their house, room after room.
In every one of them, evidence they are here
crumbs on the cloth, today's news, cups.
Near sundown I find her in the final, my
statuesque mother shrunken small. On her lap
hands folded for travel. Eyes empty as gloves.
The grove is gathering the darkness. As if it were fabric.
In the breeze the leaves clap and clap.

Rooms follow one another serial as a sentence.

About rooms there are only two times,
before and after. No staying on. I would
have it otherwise. Fabulate for you
a room where you're always
divesting beautiful shoulders.

5

Closing the Island

When I meet you again I'll be all light....

John Thompson

Elegy

for Lydia Jardine Compton

All fall from a bedroom window you watched
the turning and falling of leaves,
outwitting surgeons who foretold summer.
In November came
a warm rainy spell
              at neap tide, an offshore breeze.

In that room the Lydian measure faltered, and
those of us who were there and
those of us who came
felt the unfamiliar
of old place names.

Convolvulus

Never to have sat down at the one table
all of us, all eleven. Together,
first-born to last, a half-dozen times. Frightful
disunions, banked by floral arrangements and the obliquity
    of wreaths:
the oppressive fragrance of great grief.

Somewhere there must be a table, places set —

Will we be young there or as now orphaned adults
with lives lurking behind our chairs like footmen?
What will be the seating plan (youngest to oldest?)
and who will serve? Who, anyway,
will be able to eat seated among the mirroring faces,
the one voice made many, indistinguishable utterances.
What hunger there will be, what thirst
for completion. A part of us a continent away for years.
And will you be my brother there — not someone else's husband,
father, friend? This is the riddle
to be said five times before grace —
And will you be my sister there as you were before the world
stole you away? In the sibling riddle there are five names.
Can you come
back? Imagine
a room of pure being. History, a backpack left at the door:
entering the age before we
took passage
into strangers' lives, alien ways.

Back then
behind a house gate called Beautiful
a family, blood so thick it clotted
resemblances conceived in cousin-marriages, and perpetuated.
In the convolute double-helix
an encryption of information.

On that table, I want wild flowers, not wreaths.

In the fall I remember

an abundant life in a large house:
we were a crowd, a country, a state.
Done, doing, and yet to do — work without end,
work named by the hour, the day, and the season
a marshalled life.

My father did everything, was everything —
lord of our lives — a cursing, gentle man.
He could parse and he could scan,
line a psalm, recite a poem, build a barn.
For him we took each meal in silence
eleven children and always the visitors:
his rule.

Every room full and attics stowed
halls without heat and winter stoves:
and below
in the cool dark cellar
jars of jam, red as cardinals and gold-capped.
In the well-house, pickled hams and dried fish,
and twice a week, the baking.

A life banked against winter.

What Land Means: Autumn 1998

The Horse Chestnut dies from the bottom up
the leaf withers from the edge inward.
Until that explosive moment, your heart
kept its secret: No tatters on the summertime of your age.

Youngest sons aren't supposed to leave first.
Didn't you know that? Abandoning all.
Overtaking autumnal brothers and sisters, you fell
asleep on your feet, the quick stride stilled
between house and fields.

The last thing seen, they say, is forever held in memory.

So you could see those fields still (by times, coasted,
cultivated, cropped), we planted you
on the down slope of a hill: Advantage to all your acres,
a family loam richest in you, Great Tree. Hold me
in view. Wait at the bottom till I coast to you.
We'll climb up together. Into green branches.

Waking

On the edge of consciousness   remembered this

ten brothers and sisters in formal filial line
the length of a room
"a friggin' militia," a drunk man says, passing down the line

not still but moving
they bend their similar heads and extend their arms
like swimmers through the mourning tide:
six-foot high human wave churning the blasphemous sea

at the far end of the room candles argue solid blackness
sum line of a life

your name gusting over the riptide

the stranger weaving among us
strokes and releases
aviate condolences that flutter like scarfed pale birds

unable to rest

Inherit the Light

When we return to that island, words won't be necessary.
There will be no signposts; getting lost will not be possible.
Roads ascend and descend ripening grainfield hills.
Cardigan and Cardross will be where you find them.

Someone will bring you; another will walk you the way
and a third there will be whose face is the words to a song
    we no longer need.

Where you are is where you were going:
neither towards nor away invite you.
Arrival is already.

After this.
After the spoken world.

Index of titles

1 At the Bridge the Body Rises

North Shore, PEI	3
Men and Women, Remembered	4
plotted	5
This and That Room, June	7
4 April, 1991	8
ploughshares into words	9
Amanuensis: John Milton's Daughter	11
The Dinner Party	12
October Morning	14
Island House, November	15
Going Over the Sand Dunes	16
Night Drive, November, for her ninetieth birthday	17

2 Women Writing Men

Letter to France	21
Hester Pyrnne's Letter to Surveyor Pue	22
She Talks to Pictures at an Exhibition Because theCurator Won't Allow Notes	23
"The Mermaids Singing"	24
Guenevere Writes to Them Who Wrote of Her	25
Done with the compass, / Done with the chart	27
Tidying the Tower: The Lady of Shalott Without Tennyson	28
Rheumatic Fever: any nineteenth-century poet to her mentor	30
Tower: Poem for the Spoken Voice	31
Nine Women Come for Dinner	33
Pairs	34
Poet in His Cell	36
Do Not Write Any More	37

3 Inherit the Light

Lightwork in Vermeer	41
Ripening Grain	43
The Falling Asleep of the Virgin Mary: August 15	44
Cezanne: Still Life	45
Blinded by the Word	46
A Thin Woman Looks at Renoir's *The Bathers* 1918–19	48
Unreadable Flowers	49
Heat, August	50
Claude Monet: *Rouen Cathedral Early Morning, 1894*	51
Host	52
Crow Song, November	53
Mind Winter	55
rooms	57

4 *Body my house / my horse, my hound / what will I do / when you are fallen....*

Your House Should Be a Second Skin...	61
House on a Hill	62
Sons and Lovers	63
Landfall at High Tide Leads to Stormsurge	64
The Womb Lies Beneath the Heart	65
She Declines His Proposition	66
Features	68
The Insomniac's Lighthouse	69
Winter Dusk	70
They Hold My Coat	71
Wrist	72
shoulder blades	73
The Room Before	74

5 Closing the Island

Elegy	79
Convolvulus	80
In the fall I remember	82
What Land Means: Autumn 1998	83
Waking	84
Inherit the Light	85

Notes

PAGE 1. The epigraph to section I is quoted from Robert Kroetsch's *Seed Catalogue*.

16. "Going Over the Sand Dunes" ends with a line from the medieval ballad "The Twa Corbies."

19. In the first of the *Duino Elegies*, Rilke writes, "Not angels, not humans, / and already the animals are aware / that we are not really at home in / our interpreted world." In *Relationships*, Elizabeth Jennings' "A Sonnet" begins, "Run home all clichés, let the deep words come / However much they hurt and shock and bruise" and continues, "There are no categories for what I know...."

22. "The main facts" of *The Scarlet Letter*, Nathaniel Hawthorne writes, "are authorized and authenticated by the document of Mr. Surveyor Pue," Hawthorne's predecessor, some "fourscore years" earlier at the custom-house, which is where Hawthorne "finds" the scarlet letter, the document wrapped around it.

23. "She Talks to Pictures at an Exhibition" refers to Edgar Degas' painting *Absinthe*, 1876.

24. "Ungart'red" and so forth is Ophelia's description of Hamlet in Act II, Scene III of the play.

25. Guenevere has in mind her story as it was told by Sir Thomas Malory, in the 15th century, and by William Morris and Alfred, Lord Tennyson, in the 19th century. Malory is quoted.

30. The epigraph is from sonnet thirty-two of *Sonnets from the Portugese*, by Elizabeth Barrett Browning.

31. W.B. Yeats's poems "High Talk" and "Leda and the Swan" are quoted.

34. The reference to St. Augustine appears in Frank Kermode's review of W. H. Auden's *Lectures on Shakespeare* in the *London Review of Books*, 22 February, 2001. "If pigs had wings" is close to Lewis Carroll's phrasing in "The Walrus and the Carpenter."

39. The epigraph to section III derives from the Ninth Elegy of Rilke's *Duino Elegies*.

41. Hans Koningsberger, in *The World of Vermeer 1632–1675*, is the art critic referred to in "Lightwork in Vermeer."

44. In the calendar of *The Book of Common Prayer*, August 15, The Falling Asleep of the Blessed Virgin Mary, commemorates the day of her death.

45. "Cézanne: Still Life" draws upon Hugh McLeave's *A Man and His Mountain: The Life of Paul Cézanne*.

48. Lorenz Eitner, in *An Outline of 19th Century European Painting*, identifies Renoir's *The Bathers* (1918–19) as his "last, powerful statement of what mattered to him in art and life...." The poem draws upon that work and Walter Pach's *Renoir*.

49. Catharine Parr Traill didn't say any of this of course although, in *The Backwoods of Canada*, she did speak about the "marvellous food" to be had in native plants.

50. In Dante Gabriel Rossetti's "The Blessed Damozel," *strong, level flight* describes the motion of angels.

59. The epigraph to section four is quoted from May Swenson's "Question" in *To Mix with Time: New and Selected*.

77. The epigraph to the final section is quoted from John Thompson's Ghazal XVIII, *Stilt Jack*.